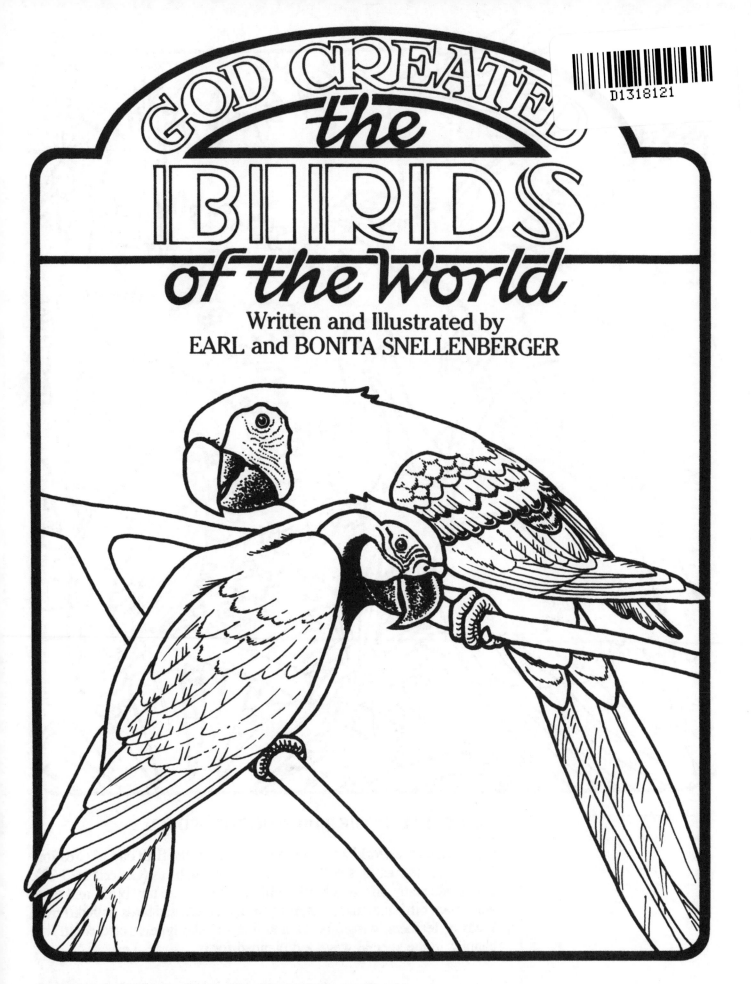

GOD CREATED the BIRDS of the World

Written and Illustrated by
EARL and BONITA SNELLENBERGER

ISBN 0-89051-152-7 Printed in China

GOD CREATED THE BIRDS OF THE WORLD.

God created the world and everything in it. On the fifth day of Creation, God made the creatures of the sea and the winged birds (Genesis 1:20-23). God made many different kinds of birds. There were tiny birds, and there were giant birds and many others as well. God created birds with different kinds of feathers, wings, beaks and feet so each type of bird could live happily in the special way God planned for it.

GOD GAVE MANKIND DOMINION OVER THE BIRDS.

After God created Adam, the first man, God brought the birds before Adam and let him name them (Genesis 2:19,20). God created a woman, Eve, to be Adam's wife. God gave mankind "dominion over" the living things He created (Genesis 1:28). That means we are to be responsible for birds and the other creatures God created. Adam and Eve must have enjoyed taking care of the beautiful and interesting birds that lived with them in their home, the Garden of Eden.

Female

Male

ALL BIRDS HAVE FEATHERS AND WINGS.

God gave feathers to the birds for several reasons. Feathers help protect birds from the sun. And feathers help birds keep warm and dry when it's cold and wet. Most birds need feathers to help them fly. God also gave birds feathers to help attract mates. This male Red-plumed Bird of Paradise from New Guinea is parading and displaying his beautiful feathers. He hopes to attract the less brightly colored female to be his mate.

4

GOD BLESSED THE BIRDS AND TOLD THEM TO MULTIPLY IN THE EARTH (Genesis 1:22).

God made a male and female of each of the different kinds of birds He created. God wanted the male and female to mate and become father and mother to baby birds. Baby birds need lots of love and attention to survive and grow. God knew that these baby Robins would need a father and mother to build a safe nest for them. Mother and Father Robin would bring them plenty of food until they were big enough to care for themselves.

BABY BIRDS GROW INSIDE THE EGGS THEIR MOTHERS LAY.

God planned for birds to multiply or reproduce in a special way. Mother birds lay eggs. When these eggs are "incubated" (kept warm by the mother or father bird's body), the baby birds grow safely inside the hard shells. The yellow yolk and white of the egg provide all the food and water this baby chicken needs as it develops. After 21 days of incubation, this chick uses its beak to break out of the shell. Perhaps you have seen a chick just after it has hatched.

A MOTHER HEN LOVES AND CARES FOR HER CHICKS.

God planned for baby birds to be cared for by one or both parents after they are hatched. A loving mother hen helps her chicks find food and water, and she keeps them safe and warm under her wings. Jesus uses the mother hen as an example of how He loves and wants to care for us. If we obediently come to Jesus as children of God, He will gather us together as a hen gathers her chicks under her wings (Matthew 23:37; Luke 13:34). Isn't that a wonderful promise?

Male

Female

THE HUMMINGBIRD LAYS THE SMALLEST EGG.

The Hummingbird is the smallest bird in the world, and it lays the smallest egg — the size of a pea! The mother Hummingbird lays two pure-white eggs in a tiny, cup-shaped nest built of plant down and spider webs. Hummingbirds' wings beat so fast they produce the humming sound that gave them their name. Only 3 1/2 inches long (8.9 centimeters), these Ruby-throated Hummingbirds hover like little helicopters. This allows them to sip sweet nectar from tubular flowers with their long beaks.

Male

Female

THE OSTRICH LAYS THE LARGEST EGG.

The African Ostrich, 8 feet tall (2.4 meters) and weighing more than 300 pounds (136.1 kilograms), is the largest bird in the world. The female Ostrich scrapes out a depression in sand for a nest in which she lays 10 to 12 of the largest eggs in the world. Each white egg is 6 to 8 inches long (15.2 to 20.3 centimeters) and weighs about 3 pounds (1.4 kilograms). God gave the Ostrich keen eyes to see approaching danger and strong legs and feet with sharp toenails to kick any predator that comes after its babies. The Bible mentions the ostrich in Job (vs. 39:13-18).

Male

Female

THE BALTIMORE ORIOLE BUILDS A COMPLICATED NEST.

God gave each bird He created the instinct or knowledge to build a special kind of nest to hold and protect its eggs and babies. The Baltimore Oriole hangs its tightly woven nest of grasses and other fibers from tree branches. As with many other birds, God made the female Oriole less colorful than the male for protection. She will not be as noticeable to predators while she is sitting on her eggs or covering her babies in the nest.

Female

Male

THE EMPEROR PENGUIN BUILDS NO NEST AT ALL.

There is no material to use for building a nest on the frozen Antarctic sea ice where the Emperor Penguins live. However, God gave the Emperor Penguin a fold of feathered skin that hangs down from its belly. When the female lays her egg, the male immediately places it on his feet and hides it under this warm apron of skin until the chick hatches. The parents then take turns holding the chick so they may fish and bring back food for the baby penguin.

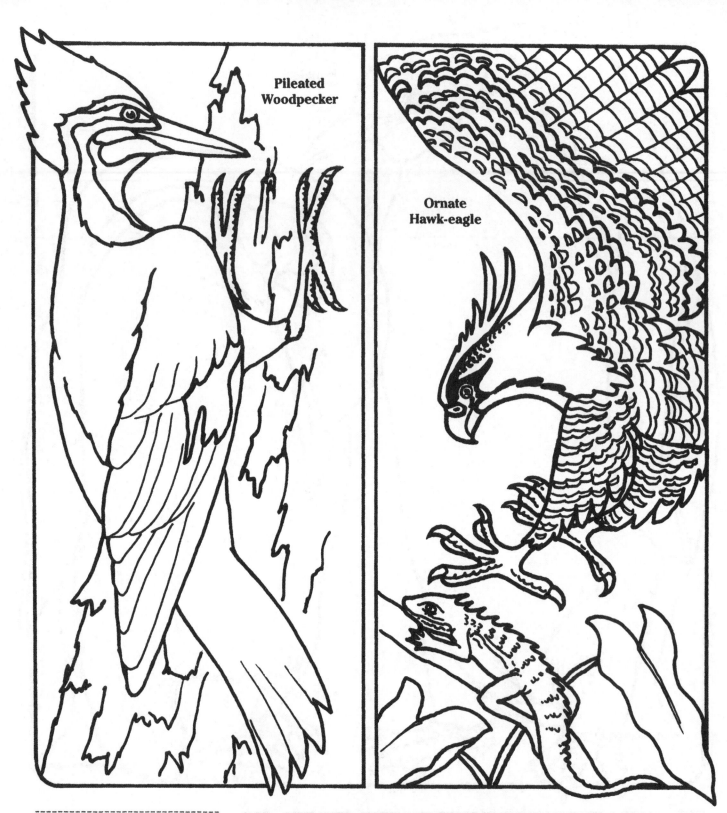

Pileated
Woodpecker

Ornate
Hawk-eagle

GOD CREATED BIRDS WITH DIFFERENT KINDS OF BEAKS AND FEET.

God gave the Pileated Woodpecker unusual feet with two toes pointed forward and two pointed backward to hook securely into the side of a tree. He put a spongy pad of tissue behind its sharp beak to absorb the shock of drilling holes to reach the wood-boring insects it eats. God gave the Ornate Hawk-eagle of Mexico large, sharp claws and a heavy, hooked beak which it uses to catch lizards and other small animals.

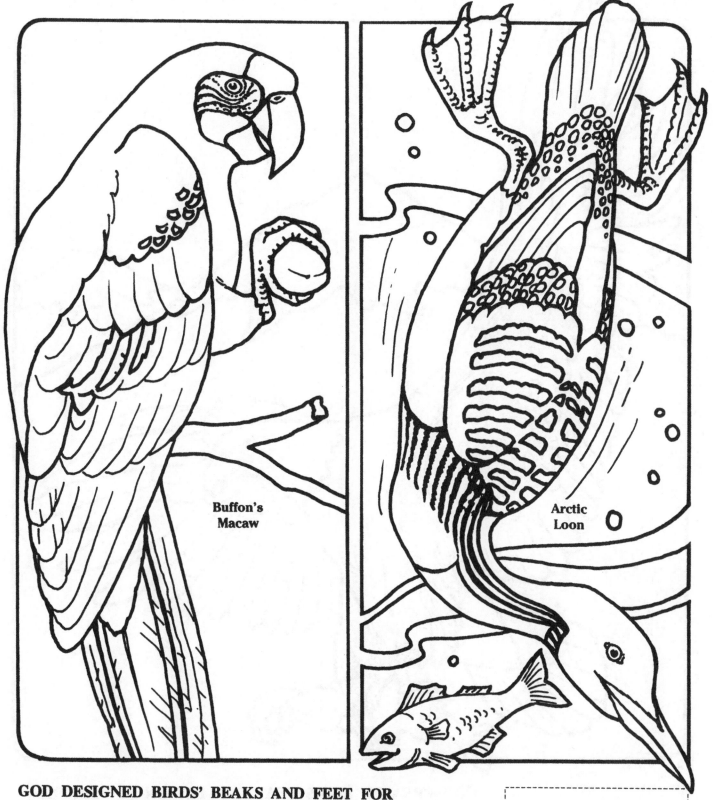

Buffon's
Macaw

Arctic
Loon

GOD DESIGNED BIRDS' BEAKS AND FEET FOR GATHERING DIFFERENT KINDS OF FOOD.

God gave parrots like the Buffon's Macaw a big, thick beak that can crack the hardest nut. The parrot is the only bird in the world that can use its foot like a hand to bring food up to its mouth. The Arctic Loon has webbed feet that stick out near the back end of its body like paddles. God knew that these feet would help it swim and dive deep under the water to catch fish with its long beak.

GOD CREATED BIRDS THAT CAN FLY ON POWERFUL WINGS.

Chosen as its national bird in 1792, the Bald Eagle is the famous symbol of the United States of America. It appears on the nation's great seal and on U.S. coins. The eagle's powerful wings carry it swiftly to its nest built on high places near rivers where it catches its favorite food, fish. God's word promises us, "They that wait upon the Lord shall renew their strength, they shall mount up with wings as eagles..." (Isaiah 40:31).

GOD CREATED BIRDS THAT CANNOT FLY AT ALL.

Like the Bald Eagle, the Kiwi also has become a symbol for a nation. The Kiwi appears on New Zealand coins, postage stamps, and the Dominion seal. Long, hairlike feathers completely hide the tiny wings of this flightless bird that is used as a trademark for shoe polish and other New Zealand products. God made the Kiwi the only bird whose nostrils open at the tip of its bill. He gave it a keen sense of smell to locate the worms and grubs it eats.

Turkey

Goose

Body Contour Feather

Flight Feather

Down Feather

Hen

3 TYPES OF FEATHERS

SOME OF THE BIRDS GOD CREATED FURNISH US FOOD AND FEATHERS.

A big turkey dinner is the traditional feast for Thanksgiving Day in the United States, but we should be thankful every day that God created birds. Chickens are delicious to eat, and their eggs are used for cooking and baking. Roast goose is tasty, and the goose's down feathers are used to make soft pillows and warm quilts. The strong flight feathers of birds were used for quill pens, and the Indians used them to make arrows.

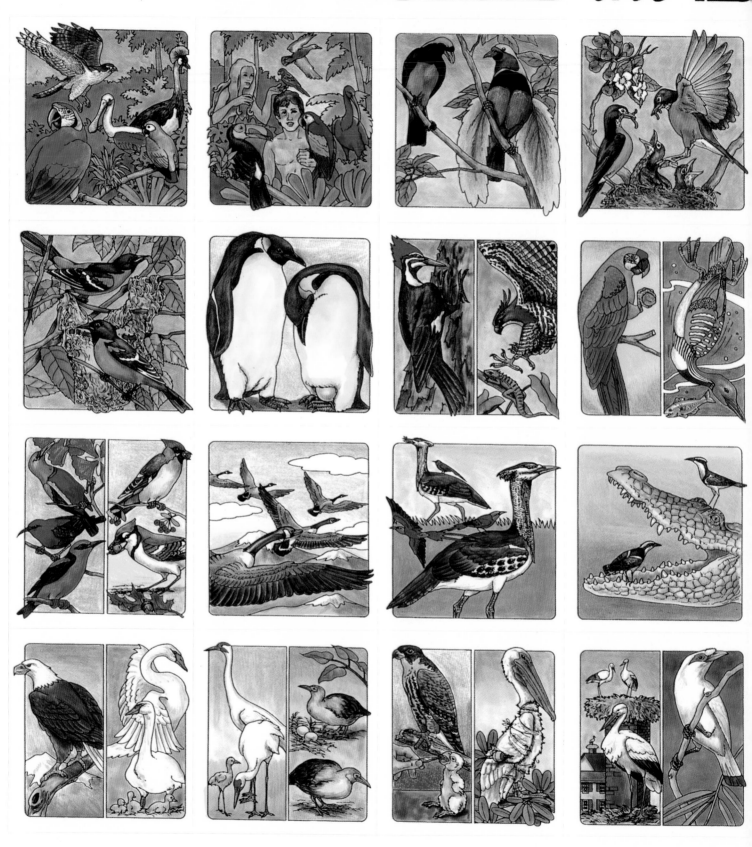

THESE 32 STICKERS SHOW THE BIRDS IN THEIR NATURAL COLORS AS GOD MADE THEM. FIND THE MATCHING PICTURE FOR EACH STICKER.

BIRDS of the World

PLACE EACH STICKER BENEATH ITS MATCHING PICTURE. YOU MAY USE
THESE STICKERS AS GUIDES FOR COLORING THE PAGES OF THIS BOOK.

Barn Swallow

California Condor

Long-eared Owl

Meadowlark

GOD CREATED BIRDS THAT HELP US BY EATING HARMFUL INSECTS AND RODENTS.

Barn Swallows swoop through the air, sweeping up great numbers of mosquitoes and flies in their wide beaks. Meadowlarks feast on crop-destroying grasshoppers. Like other owls, the valuable Long-eared Owl catches many rats and mice. Just one mouse can eat 25 pounds (11.3 kilograms) of a farmer's grain in a year. The California Condor, like other carrion birds, helps prevent the spread of disease by eating the decaying bodies of dead animals.

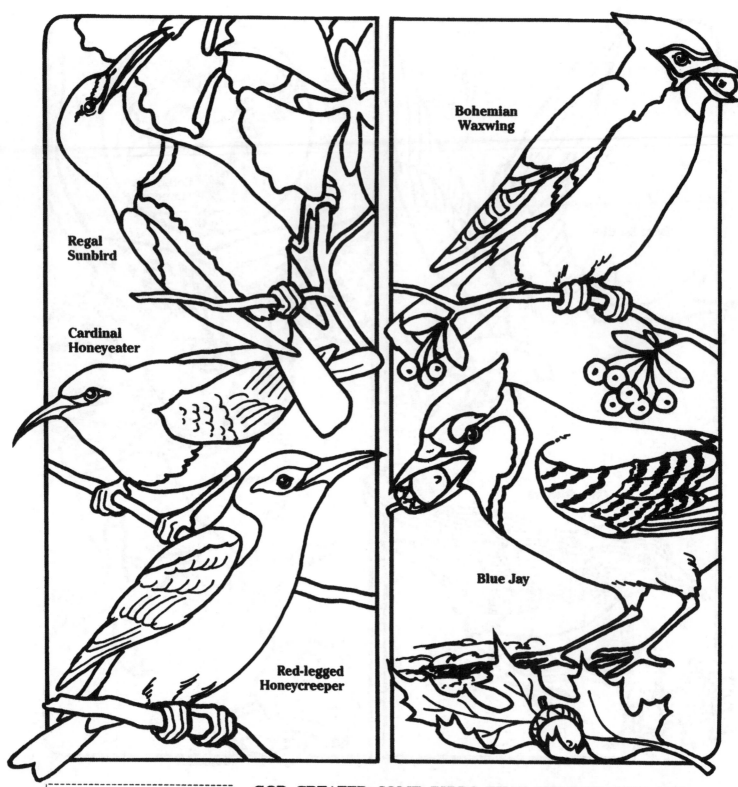

Regal
Sunbird

Cardinal
Honeyeater

Bohemian
Waxwing

Blue Jay

Red-legged
Honeycreeper

GOD CREATED SOME BIRDS THAT HELP PLANTS AND TREES REPRODUCE.

To produce seeds, many plants must have the yellow pollen dust in their blossoms transferred to the seed forming parts of the flower. This is called pollination. African Sunbirds, nectar-eating Honeycreepers of tropical America, and Australian Honeyeaters pollinate the flowers they visit. Blue Jays plant oak trees by burying acorns. By eating their berries and spreading their seeds, Waxwings help many kinds of plants reproduce.

GOD CREATED BIRDS THAT COOPERATE WITH OTHERS IN THEIR FLOCK.

God gave some birds the knowledge to migrate — to follow His directions to fly to a warmer place when the weather turns cold. "Yea, the stork in the heavens knows her appointed times, and the turtle dove and the crane and the swallow observe the time of their coming..." (Jeremiah 8:7). Migrating Canadian Geese cooperate by flying in "V" formation to conserve energy. They also make noises to keep flock members together at night or in dense clouds.

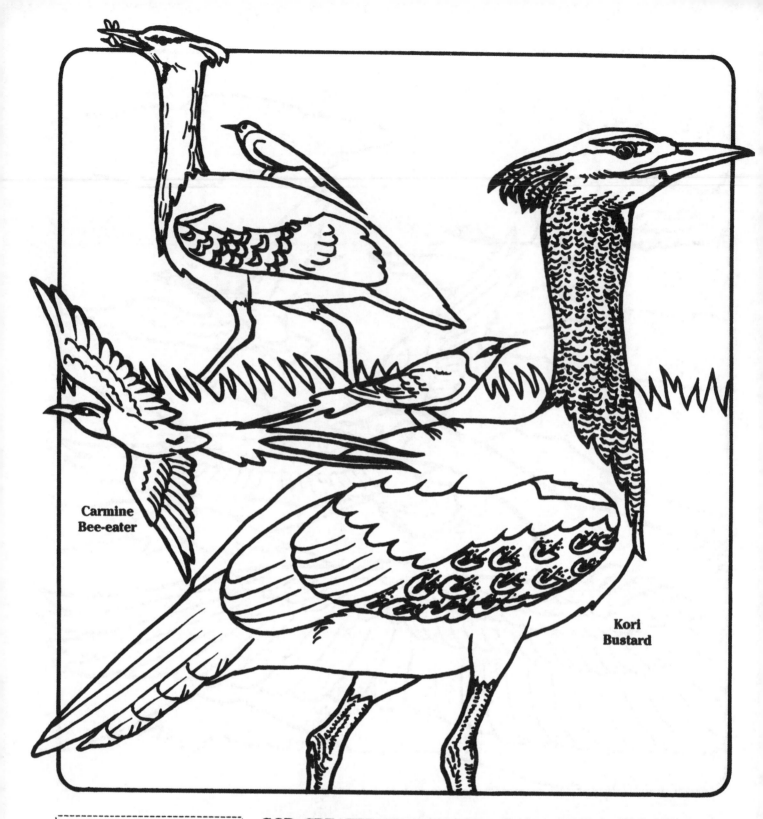

Carmine Bee-eater

Kori Bustard

GOD CREATED BIRDS THAT COOPERATE WITH OTHER KINDS OF BIRDS.

God has created relationships between two different living things where each is helped in some way. Scientists call these *symbiotic* (sym-bi-OT-ic) relationships, and two African birds have such a partnership. When the Kori Bustard goes for a walk in tall grass, the tiny Carmine Bee-eater rides on its back. From this perch, the Carmine Bee-eater darts out to catch the bees and wasps that fly up, startled by the Kori Bustard's legs and feet.

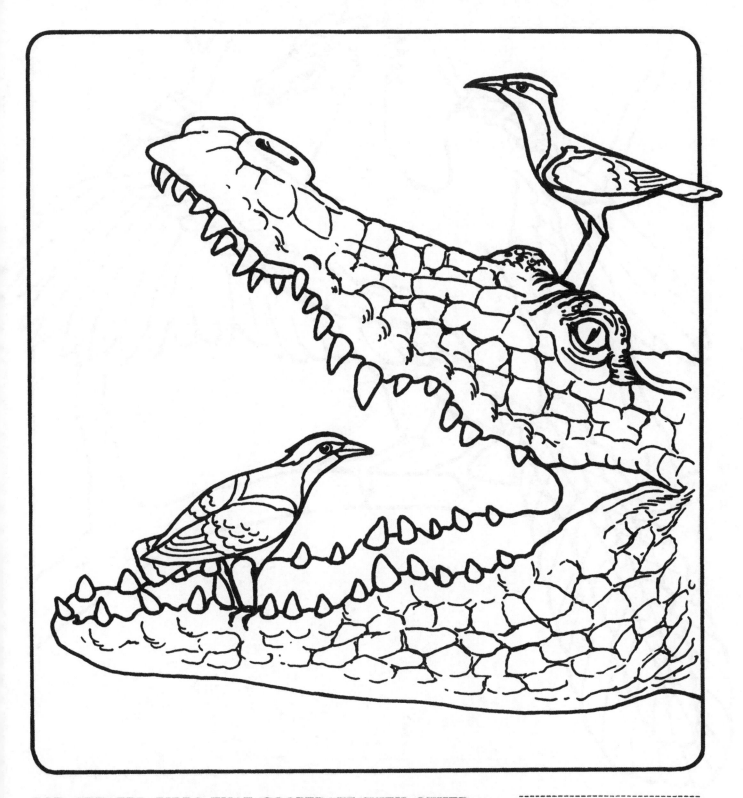

GOD CREATED BIRDS THAT COOPERATE WITH OTHER ANIMALS.

God planned for the Egyptian Plover and the Nile Crocodile to have a *symbiotic relationship*. When the huge Nile Crocodile comes out of the river to rest in the sun, it allows the Egyptian Plover to hop and climb safely all over its body even inside its sharp-toothed jaws! The Nile Crocodile is unable to reach the blood-sucking leeches that attach to the crocodile's hide, teeth and gums. The Egyptian Plover helps the crocodile by picking off and eating these leeches.

GOD CREATED UNUSUAL BIRDS THAT ARE NOW EXTINCT.

A living thing becomes *extinct* when the last of its kind dies. We know about the extinct bird Archaeopteryx (AR-ke-OP-ter-riks), meaning "ancient wing" from fossils. These fossils are the hardened remains of Archaeopteryx found in sedimentary rocks which may have been formed by the rushing waters of Noah's Flood. The unusual Archaeopteryx had claws on its wings — and teeth! What color was it? Nobody knows!

GOD CREATED UNUSUAL BIRDS THAT ARE ALIVE TODAY.

Young South American Hoatzins (ho-WATT-sins) have two sharp claws on each wing to help them climb around on vines and trees. Hoatzins build their nests in branches overhanging tropical rivers. If in danger, the chicks dive into the water and swim to safety. Hoatzins lose their wing claws when they become adults, but still use their wings climbing in dense jungle foliage. The African Turaco is another bird with "climbing claws."

Dodos

BIRDS THAT ARE NOW EXTINCT WERE ON NOAH'S ARK.

Long ago, God had a good man named Noah build a huge boat called the Ark. After Noah's family and at least one pair of every land creature, (including each kind of bird) were safely aboard the Ark, God sent the Great Flood which covered the whole earth. Although saved from the Flood, Dodos were extinct by 1680. Sailors came to the ground-nesting Dodo's Mauritius Island home and killed many birds. They also brought the pigs and rats that ate the Dodo's eggs.

Passenger Pidgeons

Great Auks

SOME BIRDS GOD CREATED HAVE BEEN OVERHUNTED TO EXTINCTION.

The Bible tells us that not a single sparrow falls to the ground in death without our Heavenly Father's knowledge (Matthew 10:29- 31). God cares for the birds He created, and it is a terrible thing when one becomes extinct. The last two Great Auks in the world were killed in 1844 to be stuffed for a wealthy man's collection. Relentless hunting made the once common Passenger Pigeon extinct by 1914.

Bald Eagle

Trumpeter Swan

ENDING THE HUNTING OF ENDANGERED BIRDS WILL HELP SAVE THEM FROM EXTINCTION.

Living things in danger of extinction are called *endangered species*. Hunting is one reason the Bald Eagle became an endangered species. Before Bald Eagles were protected by Federal law, more than 125,000 were killed in Alaska alone over a 35 year period. Trumpeter Swans, nearly extinct from overhunting, multiplied from 69 in 1935 to 10,000 today. A safe habitat was made for them at Red Rock Lakes National Wildlife Refuge in Montana.

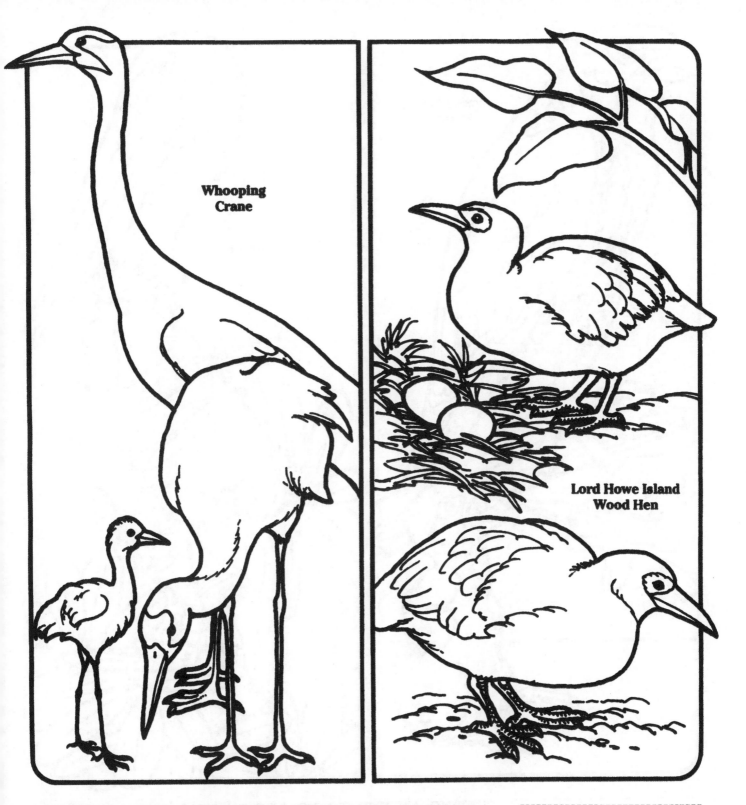

Whooping
Crane

Lord Howe Island
Wood Hen

PROTECTING THE HABITATS OF ENDANGERED SPECIES WILL HELP THEM SURVIVE.

A *habitat* is the place where something lives. Whooping Cranes nearly became extinct when their wet marshland habitats were drained for farming. Placed in protected habitats, Whooping Cranes have increased in number from 21 in 1941 to about 200 today. The Lord Howe Island Wood Hen was saved from extinction when its chief predators disappeared. The descendants of the pigs, cats and rats that were brought to its Australian island habitat by sailors nearly 200 years ago were removed.

Peregrine Falcon

Pelican

PUTTING AN END TO POLLUTION WILL MAKE THE WORLD A SAFER PLACE FOR BIRDS.

Pesticides are poisons that are sprayed on crops to kill weeds and destructive insects. A pesticide called DDT was washed by rainwater into rivers, lakes and seas where it poisoned fish. When Peregrine Falcons ate the fish, the DDT caused the shells of their eggs to be thin and break easily. Peregrine Falcon eggs are being hatched in laboratories to save these birds from extinction. Other birds have been harmed by discarded trash. Man's dominion over the earth requires a responsibility to preserve and protect God's creation. Don't pollute!

Bali
Mynah

White
Stork

CONSERVATION PROGRAMS ARE HELPING BIRDS ALL OVER THE WORLD.

A *conservationist* is someone who works to save and protect living things and their habitats. Conservationists in Europe are working to save the beloved storks that have nested on their rooftops for centuries by importing stork eggs from Africa (where the storks migrate) and hatching them in incubators. Bali Mynahs from Indonesia have been saved from extinction by raising them in zoos. Though the Bible warns us about worshiping nature, caring for and preserving God's Creation is responsible stewardship.

YOU CAN HELP BIRDS BY BUILDING HOUSES FOR THEM AND PROTECTING THEIR NESTS.

Imported from Europe, Starlings and English Sparrows have driven the gentle native Bluebird from its nesting places. You and your family can help save Bluebirds from extinction by building special nesting boxes for them. Any nesting box should be built with a specific bird in mind. A Wren box must be very different from one for a Wood Duck. There are library books that give instructions for building special kinds of birdhouses. This can be a very interesting family project.

YOUR CAN HELP BIRDS BY PROVIDING FOOD, WATER AND PROTECTION FOR THEM.

You and your parents may be able to plant shrubs, vines and trees that will provide food for birds as well as places for them to nest and hide from predators. Provide water for drinking and bathing, especially during warm months. Provide food during the winter months when it is scarce. Ask your State Conservation Department what foods are best for birds in your area.

Canary

Parakeet

BIRDS HAVE MADE WONDERFUL PETS FOR MANY YEARS.

The Bible tells us, "A righteous man regardeth the life of his beast..." (Proverbs 12:10). God expects us to take proper care of animals that are ours. Wild birds may be beautiful and interesting to watch, but you should never buy wild birds as pets. Canaries and Parakeets make excellent pets, and they have been properly raised in captivity for many years. Canaries have been popular pets since 1500 and Parakeets since World War II.